The PATH of HOPE

CHLOE TRAVISS

Tellwell Talent
www.tellwell.ca

ISBN
978-0-2288-5322-0 (Paperback)
978-0-2288-5323-7 (eBook)

INTRO

death has never been a fear in my mind. it is a time and place that i know will come. it always does. it will creep up around the corner and take you away unexpectedly. usually at the worst time possible. but no time is ever a good time to go because i know that when i go, my mind will shut off. i won't have anyone in my life anymore. my heart will stop beating, but i will never lose my love for my people. they will always be a part of me, making me the best version of myself. the incredible person i always wished to be. they've made that happen. this had all made me, me.

that is why i've made this book. in honour of remembrance. to remember the love and hope that is real and possible for others to find. to prove real, pure love does exist. when beginning to write this book, i was broken and shattered into millions of pieces, like a broken mirror smashed by what was my 'ugly' reflection. now at this point in my life, i've finally been able to find myself because of the love that my true people give me. putting me back together differently. the best difference there is.

every obstacle i've conquered, every battle i've fought through, every fire i've walked through, has helped me overcome the beginning. now let's live peacefully in bliss and never worry about what the universe still has to offer; because i can promise you this one thing, that whatever is going to take up a part of your life at any unexpected time is worth the fight because in the end, it is not about making it through the fire of this world, but how you chose to walk through and make your way out of that burning fire. Every single thing in this world was made to be temporary; love, suffering, happiness, people, loved ones, hatred and feelings. There is not a single thing that you can truly keep forever because everything's meant to venture to its own path eventually. By this being said, us people need to learn how to live in each moment like it is truly the last, because you never know when it really is the last time. The last goodbye, the last hello, the last breath, it all comes too unexpectedly, in the blink of an eye, what you once knew is no longer with you. You must take that temporary part of your life and turn it into something more. Turn it into your true self, build yourself from these experiences, feelings, and so on.

i hate that i rely on you

your presence is calming
strong enough to reduce my anxiety
i don't want to need you
making you a necessity
until the day you put me in the grave
the more i give in
the more damage is done

a divider to hide from reality

i cheated

                                        don't do it

i promise i tried

after it happened

                                        missed call

i tried to hide

don't want to remember

                                        how are you

i'm fine *i could have died*

the night's almost over

                            text me when you're home safe

thoughts so twisted and tied

voices in my head

                                    how long's the drive

time to confide

the moment came

                                    is everything okay

i smiled, nodded, and lied

guilt building up

                                            hey baby

so i broke down and cried

in so much pain

                                        talk to me

truth rolling up like an ocean's tide

the words you spoke were lies

you told me you love me more than i love you
and i believed it
until you left me heartbroken, feeling unwanted
while i endlessly waited for you to come back

if

sometimes i lay in bed thinking of you
wondering what we would be doing at this moment
if things were different
if
a supposition; uncertain possibility
that is exactly us
we are an if
an unwanted if

music

i cant listen to my old music anymore without thinking of you
fuck you for ruining my music too

addict

my addiction for your love is stronger than my addiction to nicotine
both toxic and almost impossible to quit

unhealthy craving

i felt so close to feeling sane until all of this and before
the remaining memories of you leave me craving more

top priority

even though you knew your second choice was in love with you
earlier that night you tried to kiss your top priority girl
and although that happened, you told your second choice you love her too
finally decided to give that second choice a whirl
after realizing your top priority was done with you

emotional help

ask, don't tell
help, don't watch
talk about heaven, not hell
drink water, not scotch

it's only ever when you need something

you randomly me in the a.m.
i answer the phone, you begin to weep
i you back in the p.m.
no response; you're already asleep

why

why do you always decide to fuck up mornings and nights
and leave worry to linger in my mind
the entire day

afraid to forget

sometimes i fear death
not the thought of dying in particular
but the thought of our memories being washed away
forgotten by my own mind
and i know my memories are the only things that keep me sane
so what will i do if i can't remember you

bad luck

bad time
bad place
bad choices
convenient lips
new face

rumours

---

people talk
rumours spread
like a wildfire of voices
that can never be put out

the seven deadly sins

i've taken *pride* in who i am now without you
but still *covetous* for your love
the *lust* i feel towards you
doesn't cancel out the raging *anger*
consuming my ability to love again
the *gluttony* of affection you display towards her
makes me *envy* her even more
now the *sloth* and sadness without you
has left me useless and broken on the inside and out

right (wrong) decisions

i was right to meet you
right to trust you
right to confide in you
right to fall in love with you
right to believe you loved me too
over time look at how easy it was
for all of those rights to turn into wrongs

long way down

contradicting thoughts in my mind
piled up into a mountain of disappointment
trying to slowly make my way down this slope
that seems to be as steep as a cliff

cold

---

how was i supposed to know
that when you told me you love me
it meant you just wanted to touch me
i was crazy cold
and the lies you told
made me feel warm inside
you were supposed to be my ride or die

me or her

---

you told me that it was never just a friendship
that you danced with her earlier that night
kissed me later that night
told me you love me too later that night
deeply in love with her that entire time
while knowing all along
that you always had
my undivided love

drinking by yourself

when your memories come rushing back
your thoughts become clear
and your words; harder to hear

you deserve the world

i wish i could have been
everything you deserved
treated you
how you deserved to be treated

you can't rely on others

the cause of harming yourself
is not entirely because of others
it is the constant loneliness
not loving yourself
trying to deal with your thoughts
fucking up your own mind
to the point where
you can't handle yourself anymore
you must love yourself
before you can truly love anyone else

it's not all about you

you make people feel sorry for you
trying to prove that you're 'worth' more than others
to receive more attention than others
you need to realize
that your life is not half as bad
compared to others

it's easier to write about heartbreaks

than it is to write about someone you truly love
when someone breaks you
it creates a bottomless black hole in your heart
in your mind
seeping with the dreadful memories
and their unwanted existence that lives forever within you
but when you're in love
there's not enough time in the world
to let your thoughts spill from your mind
describing how much their presence is needed and adored

stuck in my mind

blinded by the darkness
falling from the night sky
only able to see the deep outlines
of the world around me in this moment
showing the different beauty that occurs
from the day to the night
at night
details turn into a blur
of scattered thoughts
consuming my mind

continually surrounded with disasters

i'm supposed to be responsible
to for help
but i can't
i'm terrified from shock
i've seen too much to be okay
i was delicate and am now broken
i cannot seem to speak
the screams from myself
and the others around me
are suffocating me
killing me slowly from inside to out

sick and tired

---

of the knives
digging into my back
leaving me suffering
with excruciating pain
harming my delicate skin
that should be left
soft and untouched
the way it once was before

how come things change

faster than the blink of an eye
faster than the speed of light
but the lights have always been absent
and now it's becoming night
and my minds being consumed with darkness
losing patience for myself
and for others
scared
to lose lovers
and friends
waiting
for my life to crumble to the ground
rapidly
like it did before

quietly suffering

i look into the mirror
back at myself i glare
seeing someone worthless and empty
like no one's even there
i try to crack a smile
while deeply broken on the inside
i should be screaming for help
but all i am able to do is hide
i'm good at hiding my feelings
i can't let anyone know
the horrible things i'm always thinking
so i continue putting on a show

how do you expect me to be okay when;

you write about her
you lied about her
you fight about her
you told me you'd die for her
you lie and don't care
never thinking to share
your thoughts
your plans
your emotions
all you ever are is bland
your style stays the same
your desire is popularity and fame
you don't see me as special
you never put me first
why do I even need you
if I'll never be your first

why is it

you only text and me when you're feeling low
when you're bored, nothing to do, and life's a little slow
when you're fighting with your girl, saying she's nothing but a hoe
when you're all alone with nothing but a white line of a kind of snow
but when i needed you the most, you decided not to show
if things were different, where would we be
i never want to know

you can't rely on others

the cause of harming yourself
is not entirely because of others
it is the constant loneliness
not loving yourself
trying to deal with your thoughts
fucking up your own mind
to the point where
you can't handle yourself anymore
you must love yourself
before you can truly love anyone else

glass that was meant to be broken

i used to look in the mirror and not recognize the reflection
the pale, blank face staring right back
the girl i never wished to be
then you came into my life
and broke the glass mirror purposely
putting the pieces back together differently
now i look into the fragile mirror and see something different
i see the girl i've been looking for forever
you've fixed me

freedom

china bird
butterfly
soar across the moonlit sky
and there they watch a caterpillar turn
to one of their own
become a butterfly
and soar all alone

unconditional love

---

you're as pretty as a blossomed flower
and as brave as a lions roar
love is a very magical power
you are the one thing that i'm living for
together we can be invincible
we will always be united as one
our connection is a magnetic pull
through all of my losses, with you, i have won
my head is spinning, not sure what to do
people tell me to follow my heart
but i'm afraid, i don't want to lose you
what is my life made of
what is this feeling
they it love

the best kind of love

passionately pressed up against each other
helplessly gazing deep into his eyes
right in front of one another
mesmerized by this view; the colours of the universe;
trees, grass, and skies
can not elucidate the way he makes me feel
gentle and slow is the way his hands grip onto my hips
butterflies i haven't felt in forever; unreal
soft and loving he is when his lips touch my lips
butterflies in my stomach
chills traveling up my spine
his love making me able to push aside my bad addictions;
like alcohol and cigarettes, because lover, you're mine

but i can't complain

i can't get my mind off of how in love i am with you
because you're the only thought that's ever on my mind

long days and longer nights

us as ordinary people are infinite
in a moment that could never be washed away by reality
constantly feeling alive in the night
as if it were day

a second family

we're all different pieces to complete a puzzle
and because of that,
i know we will be friends forever

be you, be confident, be proud

we shouldn't have to be afraid of the people around us
we shouldn't have to fear what others say to us
we are allowed to be comfortable with our actions and words we chose;
with our outfits we wear
not hiding behind what others want us to be
society should not have a say in what we believe
there is no right or wrong to the person we become
and to who we are now
it's our lives we live that make us who we are
being controlled by others should not be an option allowed
respect others and they will respect you;
treat others the same way you want to be treated
please others the same way you wish to be pleased
it's a two-way road
requiring the effort and responsibilities of one another to succeed

uncontainable lust

you are either friends with someone,
or in love with them

reasons for change

everything was okay
until there was an us
now everything has changed
but maybe it's for the better

unanticipated desire

it's hard to tell when the line between friendship and deep feelings, or fun and lust, is crossed
often we don't realize that we are head over heels in love before it's far too late to do anything but enjoy the ride

you make me feel the best kind of high

a high that is calm and powerful like listening to the waves of an ocean wash onto the beach

a high that feels like a million butterflies fluttering through my body, giving off the most incredible tingling sensation

a high that tastes like slowly biting into the sweetest strawberry in the whole bunch

a high that smells like my favourite candle constantly lit, allowing the scent to linger in an enclosed space

a high that looks like the gloomy winter snow melting away, turning into bright spring flowers *i am your flower*

___

you are the soil to my flower
the rain to my bud
the warmth the allows me bloom
the air that i require to hold a steady breath
you are what makes me grow
in ways i never thought i could

you keep me afloat

everything you do makes me feel like i am above the water
with no struggle to try to stay up
everything you say is recorded in my mind
so every time i feel like i am drowning
i press play and continue to float

car rides

---

last night i felt infinite
with the music blasted
smiling and singing non-stop
in that moment where driving with you felt like a forever
the most breathtaking forever i could ever ask for

live in the moment, not by the minute

when you look at me
time freezes
like we're the only two people in this world
making the best out of every single moment we live

shutting down

when the time comes
for me to permanently go
for my mind to shut down
and my heart to stop beating
my love for you will still be a part of me forever
a part of me with no switch to turn it off

an escape from the world i inhabited

i wanted to be at peace
with the stars and the universe
to escape this world
be invisible forever
until i looked into your eyes
realizing they were the galaxy
i desired to escape to

new life

i used to believe i would never be like this
before i met him, never thought there was a guy i could miss
the flip side of a coin and i was the other half
never thought i would love going down this different path

love triangle

you were with my friend
i was with yours
now we're together
loved them both
but with you, it's so much more

oblivious to time

when you're stuck
feeling trapped
thinking about the bad
think about how things were
a year before this moment
and realize how much can change
in such little time

take me back

not to the warm weather
or to the sand and sea
take me back
to when it was you and me
conquering the world
each and every day

communication

the communication
between us
gives me hope
that you may forgive
even though we are both unable
to forget

forever holding on

i miss you
i miss us
the memories
they are the only thing
i hold onto
with the tightest grip possible
never letting go
never giving up

gone girl

i know you will never
come back to me
but i will always
be there for you

perfect storm

when i look at you
i see perfection
like the most beautiful storm
soothing my mind
like the sound of rain tapping on a rooftop
i guess that's why we are now distant;
not all rainstorms come with a hurricane

patience

don't force anything upon your life
just because the idea of it is appealing
everything meant to happen takes time
be patient with the universe
it will always bring you what is needed

one challenge at a time

find yourself
love yourself
before bringing another obstacle into your life

dreamer

i don't see you in my dreams anymore
because my life is my new fantasy
without you in it

the breeze passing by

the sunlight beaming down
your arms wrapped around me
your body against mine
protecting my mind from all negativity
feeling safe at this moment
with you

it's crazy

how people i know
including myself
i get sick of;
tired of their constant presence
but then there's you
and whenever i'm tired of people
and need a break from the world
i just want to be alone
alone with you

bees and honey

something so quiet and soft
can create so much pain
but if you aren't afraid to know it better than that
you can find their tender, sweet spot
and see them as beauty, rather than pain

i was trapped in a whirlpool

then you jumped in
saving me from drowning
and now we are floating
on top of soft waves
the water; calming down
as we drift along together

tilt-a-whirl

when people said life is like a rollercoaster
i didn't think they meant it to be literal
i am so unbelievably in love with you
you've turned my whole world around
and tilted me in an incredible direction
that i never thought was possible
you are my tilt-a-whirl

wow

---

i always thought i knew what love was
until i met you
and wow, i was so wrong before

falling for you

you got me stumbling
on the words i say to you
tongue tied on yours
twisted up in our love
wrapped up in your arms
trapped in my mind
stuck on the thought
of loving you

a moment can last a lifetime

you think too much
stop thinking
quit talking
for just one second
and be in this moment
with me
remember how this moment feels
and cherish it
forever

i'm so scared

scared to admit to the feelings i have for you
i don't want to ruin what we already have
but i can't help it
you're irresistible
and the energy you let off
lights up my entire mind with love and lust
i need you as my lover and bestfriend
not one or the other

i try to write about you

about us
but i can't seem to get everything out onto paper
there's just so much to tell
our love story would become a novel
and our life together has only just begun

everything is temporary

you must leave yourself behind
to allow yourself to grow and move on

I would like to give a very special thanks to the people who made this possible, who believed in me and who encouraged me throughout this entire process.

Diane Traviss
Robert Traviss
Denise Alford
Jennifer Sheehan
Murray Sheehan
Jodi Konick
Tek Ang
Paul Ruthard
Trevor Bentley
Shawn Briden
Catherine Bryenton
Tony Liut
Rick Mutton
Ally Lovick
Michael Murphy
Jeff Stralak
Rob Lutz
Maggie Lutz